The Pope an

~~~~~~~~~~~~~~~~~~~~~~~~~~~~~~~

CORRESPONDENCE,

PUBLISHED IN THE "TIMES,"

BETWEEN

LORD ARUNDELL OF WARDOUR

AND

LORD ORANMORE AND BROWNE,

WITH SOME COMMENTS BY THE *TIMES.*

KILMARNOCK:

PRINTED BY JAMES McKIE, KING STREET.

MDCCCLXV.

These Letters having appeared in the *Times* at intervals, were not all seen by some who desired to read them, and at the request of many who think that, so far as they go, they express the convictions of a large body of liberal but sincere Protestants, they are now re-published. We desire that the same liberty of opinion we claim shall be extended to all, but we will use our most earnest endeavours to prevent the Church of Rome abusing our tolerance to the gradual re-establishment of her intolerant and, as we believe, baneful system.

Lord ARUNDELL has requested me to state that "he considers the statements of 'Tribune' inaccurate and irrelevant to the issue raised except in the single instance of a garbled quotation (garbled by some one) from a Papal Allocution."

CORRESPONDENCE.

THE POPE AND THE QUEEN.

TO THE EDITOR OF THE TIMES.

SIR,—Your article in the Times of this morning conveys the idea that you are not aware of the grounds upon which the Catholic body drink the toast of "Pius IX." before the toast of "The Queen." Having occasionally presided at Catholic meetings when this has been done, I may assert that it is only upon the distinction between the spiritual and the temporal, and the superiority of the one order over the other.

So far from attempting any conflict of jurisdiction as between one Sovereign Prince (a foreign Prince) and another (our own Sovereign), it presupposes that each has his own sphere, but that the sphere of one is superior to that of the other. Undoubtedly there sometimes will be a conflict of jurisdiction as between the spiritual and the temporal, principally on the debatable ground surrounding education and the family, and when it occurs it is likely, I hope, that Catholics will be found to side with God rather than man, and obey the dictates of conscience rather than the mandates of the State. The sentiment is as old as Christianity, and as inveterate as martyrdom. It is not exclusively maintained by Catholics, but by Protestants, whenever their persuasions attain the strength of principles and convictions. It was conspicuously asserted by the Non-jurors, and, indeed, the traditional toast of "Church and State" as plainly involves it as the Catholic custom of drinking the Pope's health before the Queen's. Your theory would expunge the idea of martyrdom altogether, and (however intended) is tacitly a reproach to the conduct of the early Christians themselves. On the other hand, however my sentiments may be characterized by my countrymen, I shall continue to regard myself as a good citizen on the ground that I am upholding the only principle which vindicates the dignity of the individual and prevents his absorption into the State, as in the Pagan times; and that I am adhering to the only power which has been able to rescue the individual from the omnipotence of the State, and which alone at this moment opposes itself to the centralization of governments and kingdoms, which is the tendency of modern times, and which is the natural consequence of that "Statolatrie" which is again becoming the passion of mankind.

I am, Sir, your obedient servant,
ARUNDELL OF WARDOUR.

Brown's Hotel, Dover Street, Aug. 21.

THE POPE AND THE QUEEN.

TO THE EDITOR OF THE TIMES.

SIR,—Perhaps you will allow space for a few remarks on Lord Arundell of Wardour's letter. His statement, "Undoubtedly there sometimes will be a conflict of jurisdiction as between the spiritual and temporal, principally on the debatable ground surrounding education and the family; and when it occurs, it is likely, I hope, that Catholics will be found to side with God rather than man, and obey the dictates of conscience rather than the mandates of the State," means simply that, when the interests of the Pope or the Roman Catholic Church are concerned, the authority of the Queen, or of the law of the land, lose their influence with every Roman Catholic; and as there are very few matters, whether public or private, in which the Roman Catholic Church does not interfere, I cannot see that much reliance can be placed on the allegiance of her followers. Lord

Arundell clearly enunciates the creed of the Roman Catholics, and as they thus cease to be free agents and become only part of a great machine for crushing out all freedom of thought or action, many Protestants think, as I do, that it is dangerous to encourage, or even allow, the full development of a system, which is so antagonistic to the whole spirit of the English Constitution—a system, the shackles of which were cast off by this country at no small cost. Lord Arundell again says that this sentiment is not exclusively maintained by Roman Catholics, but by Protestants, &c. True, the religious convictions of Protestants often lead them to act in opposition to the State; but there are several reasons why the State should treat such convictions differently when held by Protestants and Roman Catholics. For, with Protestants they result from their own convictions, while with Roman Catholics they are but the decree of the Pope or the Roman Catholic Church. Again, Protestants are divided into many small bodies; and even if the convictions of one of these leads it to act in opposition to the State, it is not strong enough to be dangerous. How different is the action of the Roman Catholic Church, with its 50,000 priests in Europe acting as one man, and directed by a foreign head whose interests must be always in opposition to the Protestant and liberal policy of England! In England and Scotland Roman Catholicism is in so small a minority that it assumes a milder form; in Ireland, where it is now nearly dominant, the ill-working of the system is hourly felt in its attempt to dictate in all public or private affairs. Only he who wears the shoe knows where it pinches, and it is only those who, in self-defence, live in a state of constant conflict with Roman Catholic policy who can feel how sincerely every liberal-minded man believes it to be his first duty to give it his most strenuous opposition.

I am, Sir, your obedient servant,
ORANMORE AND BROWNE.

Troon, Scotland, Sept. 6.

THE QUEEN AND THE POPE.

TO THE EDITOR OF THE TIMES.

SIR,—Lord Oranmore replies temperately to my letter, but his thought is not as cool as his diction. If Lord Oranmore had read the letter which you did me the favour to insert calmly and dispassionately, he would have seen that its fundamental idea was that the sphere of the spiritual and temporal is distinct, that any collision, therefore, between the Pope and the Queen on any purely *temporal* question was now inconceivable, but that, " as between the spiritual and temporal, &c." (the sentence which Lord Oranmore detaches from its context), conflicts of jurisdiction were occasionally to be expected, " principally on the debatable ground surrounding education and the family." This is so true that it will be very difficult for Lord Oranmore to point to any serious conflict between the Papacy and the State during the last 200 years which has not had reference simply to the freedom of its spiritual action, either as regards the laity in questions affecting family and the education of youth, or as regards its own hierarchy in the appointment of bishops, or in the freedom of its communication with them. Lord Oranmore supposes that the whole hierarchical organization of the Church has reference to a great conspiracy against the State, and he has a vision of 50,000 priests working incessantly towards this end. We, on the contrary, know that it has merely reference to the salvation of souls, and that wherever the Church is left free in its spiritual action there will be no collision with the State, and I bring it to this test,—point out in any of the multifarious contests of the Church with the State in modern times with Catholic or Protestant Governments one instance in which the Church has claimed the right to interfere on a purely political question!

I speak of modern times, and I take the last 200 years, because it is only within that period that the old polity of Europe may be said to have expired, and with that polity the claim of the Church to interfere in any secular disputes between sovereign princes. But it must not be forgotten that the deposing power arose out of the circumstances of Europe in the Middle Ages, and has died out in an altered state of things; but, whether the right was regarded as directive merely, or as an exercise of temporal jurisdiction, it was *then* alike unassailable. If as directive—*i.e.*, consultative, the Pope clearly was in his right to decide on the cases referred to him; or, if as an exercise of temporal jurisdiction—*i.e.*, of a power arising out of the maxims and usages of the Continental Law of Europe, the Pope merely exercised an authority recognized by the opinions and sentiments of the Middle Ages, universally Catholic, and which accrued to him as a right with its exercise, and which, moreover, is fully explained by the circumstances and necessities of the times, and is amply vindicated by enlightened Protestant writers, such as Liebnitz, Voight, and Hurter. "*Mais nous parlons d'Adam et d'Eve.*" Such a state of things belongs altogether to the past, and can only revive as a phantom to an excited imagination. If the Church was aggressive once, the State is aggressive now, and tends to become, to borrow Lord Oranmore's phrase, "a great machine for crushing out all freedom of thought and action," and would, if unchecked by the spiritual influence, absorb the individual, the family, the association, and mould them all to its own type and pattern. Therefore, as a politician, I am opposed to "Statolatrie," and even were I not a Catholic I should feel inclined, looking to the political tendencies of the age, favourably to regard the action of the Church as the only effectual barrier to the encroachments of the State. (*Vide* chapter on "Individual Liberty," in Balmer's *Protestantism and Catholicity Compared, in their Effects on Civilization.*)

Lord Oranmore appeals to his experience of Ireland, where an anomalous state of things exists. He may find there a political power exercised, and occasionally violently exercised by the clergy, which cannot be justified on any theory of the perfect relations of Church and State. I can only defend it in the same way that Lord Oranmore would probably proceed to defend the Established Church in Ireland, as a state of things which has its explanation and justification in the past history of Ireland. Circumstances arising out of political legislation have given the clergy in Ireland political influence which they have as much right to exercise as the Prince Bishops of the Rhine, or the Archbishop of Upsal and his clergy in the Swedish Diet.

There is an assumption throughout Lord Oranmore's letter that Catholics are incapable of the same independence of mind on political questions as Protestants. This is an assertion which I hardly like to characterize, but against it I appeal to the diversity of opinion on all possible subjects among individual Catholics out of the sphere of what is spiritual and of faith This diversity is so great that it has to be accounted for from a totally different point of view, and I will accordingly refer Lord Oranmore to Dr. Newman's lecture *Differences among Catholics no Prejudice to the Unity of the Church.*

If my letter has not already trespassed to too great a length, may I be allowed to say that, so far as it is a question of taste, I should be opposed to the Pope's health being proposed at any purely secular meeting of Catholics, and that, in fact, it is only proposed at meetings having reference to ecclesiastical objects, such as the opening of the Church at Leamington, where, I contend, it was only natural and appropriate ?

I am, Sir, your obedient servant,

ARUNDELL OF WARDOUR.

Wardour Castle, Sept. 9.

THE QUEEN AND THE POPE.

TO THE EDITOR OF THE TIMES.

SIR,—By some omission I did not see Lord Arundell's letter in your impression of the 12th till the 17th, and consequently could not reply to it till to-day. I will pass by Lord Arundell's conclusion "that my thought is not as cool as my diction," as I am at a loss to know whence this deduction, and ask you kindly to give place for a short reply to his letter. Referring to his former letter, I find that it was impossible to claim more strongly than he did that in case of any conflict between civil and religious authorities every conscientious Roman Catholic would obey the latter.

He does not now demur to that, but asks me to point out an instance within the last two centuries in which the Church has claimed the right to interfere in a *purely* political question. Here we come at once to the pith of the matter. What is *purely* political? The Church of Rome always claims to decide what is spiritual and what is political, and naturally includes in the former all that touches her own interests or policy.

Your space is too valuable, and the patience of your readers quite unequal to the perusal of an abstract of the history of the Church of Rome during the last two centuries; but perhaps you will allow me room for a few instances in the present day, where, directly or indirectly, she had taken no small part in the political affairs of Europe. From 1850 to the present, in Piedmont first and since in Italy, see her struggle against liberty with a Roman Catholic Government and people. It is probable in such a case that Lord Arundell dreads "Statolatrie." She lent the Emperor of the French no little assistance to mount the throne. Her influence with him contributed much to bring on the Crimean war, and now her power is, perhaps, the greatest difficulty the Emperor has to contend with.

Did she in no wise conduce to the late unfortunate struggle in Poland?

From her interference in Belgium has not constitutional government been almost brought to a standstill, and the very existence of her nationality imperilled?

And that "anomalous state of things" that exists in unfortunate Ireland. Are not nationality and unmitigated hostility to the English Government and people preached from almost every Roman Catholic pulpit in Ireland? Probably Lord Arundell will deem that the Roman Catholic Church exercises a beneficial influence in some or all of these cases; but, be that as it may, I think that I have shown that there are few matters of political importance in Europe in which the Roman Catholic Church does not interfere, while the influence of any Protestant Church is entirely local.

Lord Arundell seems hurt that I should assume "that Roman Catholics are incapable of the same independence of mind on political questions as Protestants;" but surely it requires little proof to show that a fish once entangled in a net rarely escapes, or that a man who has submitted his own judgment to that of the Roman Catholic Church cannot be as free to think or act as one who is untrammelled by her decisions.

Too much of past and present history is unfortunately occupied in narrating the struggles of conscientious Roman Catholics against the unceasing interference of the Roman Catholic Church, both in public and private, and I am, therefore, fully aware that many Roman Catholics, yielding to the influences of a liberal education, do exercise great independence of judgment (and I myself have benefited by it). But the Roman Catholic Church does not regard such of her sons with much favour; in former times they paid dearly for showing such independence, and now undergo no slight amount of petty persecution.

In conclusion, I must be allowed to congratulate Lord Arundell on his feelings as an Englishman overcoming so far his Roman Catholic sympathies as to make him acknowledge the bad taste of drinking the health of the Pope before that of our gracious Sovereign.

I remain, Sir, your very obedient servant,

ORANMORE AND BROWNE.

Troon, Sept. 19.

THE IRISH DIFFICULTY.

TO THE EDITOR OF THE TIMES.

SIR,—If I ask to continue my discussion with Lord Oranmore and Browne it is not in the expectation that we shall materially influence each other's opinions, but in the hope that our antagonistic views may at least come out clearly, and that there may be no haze or misconstruction between us.

Lord Oranmore insists that I assert that "in case of any conflict" between "the civil and religious authorities" every "conscientious Catholic" would obey the latter. I did not even equivalently assert that. I contemplated merely the debatable ground as it lies at this moment, "principally surrounding education and the family," and I intimated my opinion that these were legitimately within the jurisdiction of the Church. I might contemplate a very different state of things—such as might exist in hypothesis, but not in fact, although I fear it haunts the imagination of Lord Oranmore as an imminent probability—in which the Church might be supposed to aim some blow at our power or our liberties, in which I unhesitatingly declare I should side with England against any such misdirection of spiritual influence. I as distinctly, however, maintain that such a contingency is now inconceivable. I must beware lest I fall into a traditionary pitfall. Many a well-meaning and true-hearted man has been hung, drawn, and quartered upon this question, which was commonly put to Catholics under the penal laws in order to entrap them,—"If the Pope were to attack the Queen (Elizabeth), how would you act?" If they said with the Queen, they were misconstrued to recognise her supremacy; and if with the Pope, they were accused of treason to the State. But I said that since the old polity of Europe has died out such a contingency is no longer even conceivable—the sphere of the spiritual and temporal being recognised as distinct. Lord Oranmore truly demurs that the whole gist of the matter is to discover what is *purely* political. The Church claims to decide what is *spiritual*—the State claims to decide what is political ; and hence there arises, and will arise, a conflict in one form or another to the end of time.

The practical point for statesmen who rationally fear the encroachments of the Church is to discover the *animus* of the Church and her determining motive. If her aim is temporal aggrandisement, if her organization is one great conspiracy against the State, it cannot be difficult to detect this motive in her contests with the State: and therefore I contend that the matter is fairly brought to a test if, in two centuries, you cannot discover a single aggression having for its motive this greed of dominion, and which shall be judged to be so actuated by men of plain sense, who know the facts. And if no such instance can be brought forward, then I argue that there will be no conflict between the Church and the State so long as the Church, as in England, is left free in its spiritual action.

Now, what are the facts which Lord Oranmore adduces ? Lord Oranmore says, "She has taken no small part in the politics of Europe." As if it were possible for the spiritual head of 250,000,000 Catholics, *ex hypothesi*, not to take a part in the politics of Europe so long as there are debatable questions between her and the State. Precisely because, indirectly, her influence was so great, Napoleon I. said that a quarrel with her was "*une grande maladresse.*" This influence weilded by one man alarms a certain class of weak-minded politicians, and accordingly they take precautions against it by fettering the Church within her legitimate domain; whereupon begins a conflict in which either the ecclesiastical influence becomes paramount or the State gains a still more disastrous victory. The whole question is, on whose side are the encroachments and aggressions?

The patience of your readers certainly would not be equal to the retrospect of 200 years, but would be refreshed by one telling instance of purely political aggression. Lord Oranmore instances the treatment of Piedmont. Piedmont ! Who troubled the waters at Castelfidardo—the lamb or the wolf ? " Or, if we go to the origin of the dispute, or at least to the three ostensible grounds of the quarrel, what were the Siccardi laws? Laws passed in violation of the existing concordates, which abolished the ecclesiastical tribunals, and suppressed certain religious festivals. What led to the exile of the Archbishop of Turin? His refusal of the sacrament to the Minister Santa Rosa. What was the nature of the Bill confiscating the property of the monasteries and suppressing certain religious orders? Was all this within the legitimate sphere of the spiritual or the temporal?

As to Poland, I beg Lord Oranmore to read the Pope's Encyclical Letter, the summary of which was in your impression of the 21st, which authoratively defines the extent to which the Pope has interfered.

Lord Oranmore's third instance is Belgium. What is the Church struggling to obtain in free Belgium? Simply the liberty of creating charitable foundations, and the agitation is not against a simple act of mortmain, but against a law which forbids any foundation without the direct and special authorization of the Executive power, and which, in case of contravention, confiscates the legacy to the profit of the Bureau of official Benevolence.

These are Lord Oranmore's only instances; but I have since read an article with which you have honoured our correspondence, in which you adduce the additional instance of the establishment of the hierarchy in England. Let me only say that the defence at the time was that it was simply an exercise of spiritual jurisdiction, and has anything since transpired to make it appear that any interference with the State or with temporalities was contemplated?

You also refer to concordats as attesting the fact of the collision between the Church and the State. Undoubtedly; but do not they also establish the recognition of the temporal jurisdiction by the Church, and the limitation of the contest to the details which are the matter of the adjustment?

But I am disheartened at the prospect of continuing this discussion when I find the only impression left upon Lord Oranmore is that I intend in future to drink the health of the Queen before the Pope's, in the face of this whole discussion and of my plain words, that although I should not propose it at a lay meeting, I thought that at meetings for ecclesiastical objects it was natural and appropriate." Thanking you for the hearing you have given me,

I am, Sir, your obedient servant,

ARUNDELL OF WARDOUR.

Wardour Castle, Sept. 23.

THE POPE AND THE QUEEN.

(FROM THE "TIMES.")

Our readers will have perused with some interest the controversy maintained in our columns by two Peers of the realm touching the practical loyalty of the Roman Catholic body. Lord Arundell of Wardour could not rest under the insinuation that the English Romanists held a divided allegiance, that they owned a duty to the Pope of Rome as well as to the Queen of Great Britain, and that in a conflict of these obligations they might possibly place the Queen below the Pope. He proceeded, therefore, to explain and dilute an allegation which could not wholly be denied, by simply claiming for Catholics that reservation of obedience which would be recognized by Christians of every profession. That we should obey God rather than man is certainly an unobjectionable proposition, but it was long since elucidated by the comment that when we venture to disobey men placed in lawful authority we ought to be very sure that we are obeying God. This assurance a Protestant would be apt to take from his conscience, but a Roman Catholic from his priest; and so in the end it might fall out, as Lord Oranmore had asserted, that "when the interests of the Pope or the Roman Catholic Church are concerned, the authority of the Queen or of the laws of the land lose their influence with every Roman Catholic." This position, however, Lord Arundell attacked by replying that the conflict of duties supposed could not in the present day occur, except under conditions which would justify the Romish view of the case; for that the sphere now claimed for the Pope's authority was so purely spiritual and unworldly that no worldly jurisdiction could suffer from the claim. Lord Oranmore yesterday put in his rejoinder, and thus rests the question between the two Peers.

We think that as far as theory is concerned Lord Oranmore has the best of the argument; indeed, we need only carry our eyes through Lord Arundell's reservations to see how large an extent of ground they might be made to cover. When it is admitted that the "freedom of spiritual action" claimed by the Romish Church comprehends independence of the State in "questions affecting family and the education of youth, and as regards the Papacy's own hierarchy in the appointment of Bishops, or in the freedom of its communication with the m,' and when these pretensions are illustrated by the voluminous lessons of experience, we are at no loss to see that the exceptions might easily counter-balance the rule. It is not only possible, but absolutely certain, that a "spiritual" jurisdiction thus defined might come into collision with a temporal jurisdiction as it would be defined by Englishmen generally. Lord Arundell contracted the meaning of the term "temporal," and expanded that of the term "spiritual," till the scope of one clashed with the scope of the other. He admits that the Popes did once claim temporal authority within independent realms or in European questions, but asserts that for the last two centuries they have dropped the pretension, and that it is nowso obsolete as to be not worth quoting. But this is only true within limits. It is true, certainly, that the Pope did not pretend the other day, as he might have done five hundred years ago, to decide the question of the Danish Duchies or to adjudicate on the claims of Germany. But, as Lord Oranmore showed, there have been many purely political questions of late in which the Pope has certainly not been inactive, though his action was not exactly that of a mediæval Pontiff. Lord Arundell will recollect, no doubt, that the Parliamentary division on this very question of Denmark was notoriously influenced, and might possibly have been decided, by directions from Rome.

On this, however, his Lordship would remark that Protestants act in the same manner, and that Anglicans, Wesleyans, or Presbyterians might combine to promote or oppose any legislation even indirectly affecting the presumed interests of their respective communions. He might say, also, that these several bodies, and especially the Non-conformists, would claim to regulate their internal affairs according to their several organizations. The Kirk of Scotland debates the admissibility of organs into churches without any appeal to the State, and Baptists and Independents are in like manner constantly deciding questions which arise within their own communions. Why should not Roman Catholics do the same without incurring the suspicion of disloyalty or double-dealing? We answer that between the cases proposed there is no practical parallel. If Rome confined her jurisdiction to questions bearing exclusively on internal doctrine or discipline, there would be no jealousy of her pretensions. To take, for instance, a case really parallel, it was quite allowable that Rome should teach Roman Catholics, whether in England or elsewhere, what to believe about the Immaculate Conception without any reference to the State. That was an exercise of authority which no Government would desire to interfere, but the claim to such an authority is something very different from the claim to create an Archbishopric of Westminster. We need hardly enter further into this matter. Lord Arundell very well knows that even in what are termed Ages of Faith, when everybody was a Catholic, and there was no Protestantism, the Kings of England and the Parliaments of England were perpetually compelled to protest and legislate against the encroachments of the Pope of Rome. He knows that at the Reformation itself the real uprising of the kingdom was not against religious doctrines, but against that very "spiritual jurisdiction" which he defends as so innocent and reasonable; nor can he forget that Roman Catholic Governments at this very day are fain to make terms at intervals for the confinement within moderate bounds of an interference which disturbs and impedes the regular administration of the State. A concordat is simply an instrument by which the Sovereign of a country comes to terms with a foreign Power and purchases as cheaply as he can the good behaviour of the intruder within his realm. It is simply irrelevant to compare with such pretensions as these the claims of Methodists or Quakers to regulate their own costumes or jubilee.

The truth is that Rome has once been all that some people think her to be now, and that what she has once been she never forgets. To take what Lord Arundell considers his strongest illustration, we have no doubt that if the state of society and knowledge would admit it, Rome would again pretend to be the arbitress in all international questions, and though, with her traditional sagacity, she measures her demands by her position, and is content now to ask for a purely "spiritual" sphere, yet that pretension, on the first favourable opportunity, would be so suddenly expanded that nobody could tell what it may contain. We draw no illustration from the state of things in Ireland, being well content to receive Lord Arundell's acknowledgment that it is "anomalous," and even occasionally unjustifiable, but we very much fear that "freedom of spiritual action" as understood at Rome would exhibit much the same features in this country if it were left with as little control. That it is controlled and reduced to innocuous proportions we believe to be due not only to the resolute and formidable Protestantism of the nation, but to the patriotic and moderate spirit of that small class of old English Catholics which Lord Arundell represents. It is in practice, not in theory, that Romanism in this country becomes tolerable. The theory is unchanged, but the practice acquires a very different aspect when expressed in the actual conduct of educated Englishmen. Over such a class Rome may still pretend to a speculative authority, but she would not be likely to try it with any mandate which a good subject should refuse to obey.

THE QUEEN AND THE POPE.

TO THE EDITOR OF THE TIMES.

SIR,—As it is your part at once to discuss topics that are of general interest, and at the same time by elucidating to guide public opinion in a right channel, I was grateful for your admitting the correspondence between Lord Arundell and myself, and well satisfied by your deeming it deserving of the able summary contained in your leading article, which said so much in reply to Lord Arundell so much better than it was in my power to express it, and therefore I should have preferred to leave it there; but, as Lord Arundell has thought well to continue it, with your usual liberality I trust you will yet kindly insert another last word.

Our correspondence must be somewhat wearisome, because, to keep to my point, I have to reply to many of Lord Arundell's statements by reiteration. Lord Arundell complains of my insisting that he asserts that in case of any conflict between the civil and religious authorities every conscientious Catholic would obey the latter, and says, "I did not even equivalently assert that," &c. I must only again copy Lord Arundell's own words. "Undoubtedly there will sometimes be a conflict of jurisdiction between the spiritual and the temporal, principally on the debatable ground surrounding education and the family, and when it occurs it is likely, I hope, that Catholics will be found to side with God rather than man, and obey the dictates of conscience rather than the mandate of the State." This sentence speaks for itself, and, I believe, conveys clearly the demands made by the Roman Catholic Church on those who acknowledge her authority.

I am sure that as an Englishman Lord Arundell would, as he states, "if he believed the Roman Catholic Church were to aim some blow at our liberties, side with England," &c.; but from the views he expresses as to such interference in other countries I hardly know *when* he would consider "the misdirection of spiritual influence to begin."

Touching Piedmont, Lord Arundell asks, "Who troubled the waters of Castelfidardo, the wolf or the lamb?" I can only reply that the lamb in this case had decidedly not only put on the wolf's clothing, but was also affected by some of his gormandizing propensities: for what caused the revulsion in Piedmont against the Roman Catholic Church? Simply that through her *spiritual* influence she had absorbed (I am told) nearly one-third of the landed property of that country, which she held free of taxes. And not only were *her clergy* liable to be tried in all cases solely by ecclesiastical tribunals, but they had the right to withdraw from the civil courts *all* causes whatever that appeared to them to involve ecclesiastical interests. It is true that these privileges were secured them by a Concordat, but naturally a people awakening to their own rights and liberties would no longer tolerate the existence of such crying abuses. Santa Rosa, as the minister of the Crown, carried measures through Parliament abolishing them, and because he acted the part of a Liberal and constitutional Minister the last sacraments of the Church were refused to him on his death-bed, and this by direct order of Fradzone, Bishop of Turin. I ask, with Lord Arundell, "Was all this within the legitimate sphere of the spiritual or temporal?"

As to Poland, I beg Lord Arundell to read your leading article on the Pope's encyclical letter.

Lord Arundell states " that the difficulty in Belgium consists simply as to the liberty of creating charitable foundations "—a mild way, as Roman Catholics know, of working on the weaknesses of mankind to transfer their property from themselves and their families to the Roman Catholic Church.

Lord Arundell deems that only weakminded politicians fear this influence. How is it exercised wherever the Roman Catholic Church has power—in Rome, in Austria, in Spain, in Peru, in Canada, &c.? It is, I think, rather a weakminded politician who will " cast aside experience and trust to theory," or will accept the Roman Catholic Church as the friend of enlightenment, charity, and goodwill in England, when he has but to look to any part of the globe in which her influence is paramount and see whether, now as ever, she does not make religion a stepping-stone to power, the most absolute, and in many instances the most injurious, that ever held in thraldom the mind of man, or swayed the destinies of so large a portion of the human race.

I remain, Sir, your very obedient servant,

ORANMORE AND BROWNE.

Troon, Scotland, Sept. 28.

THE QUEEN AND THE POPE.

TO THE EDITOR OF THE TIMES.

SIR,—A prolonged excursion upon the Continent out of the usual track of English travellers have prevented my meeting with any English journals for nearly three weeks, it is only within the last few days I have perused the letter of Lord Arundel, and the replies to the same elicited from Lord Oranmore which at different periods have appeared in " The Times."

The controversy, commencing with the subject of the offensive and disloyal toast, which originating, as might have been expected, among the Romish priesthood in Ireland, and which was in that country at least openly avowed as intended to exhibit the Papal authority superior to that of the Sovereign of the British realm, has eventually diverged into other subjects more or less connected with it, particularly the present state of Roman Catholicism in its relations to civil and political power and authority both in England and Ireland, as well as upon the continent.

Of the class of which Lord Arundell is a member—the noble old English Roman Catholics—I have no wish to speak otherwise than with the most profound respect. Their steadfast loyalty to their Sovereign and country, their dignity under privation and misfortune, and their probity and honour in all the transactions of ordinary life, have been almost universally acknowledged, even by those most opposed to their religious opinions. His Lordship, however, must permit me to observe that the style and tenour of his recent correspondence has not been of a nature to lessen that distrust of his co-religionists which during the last 20 years has gradually arisen, unhappily not without some degree of reason both in England and upon the Continent, not merely among Protestants, but in the minds of Liberal-Conservative Roman Catholics themselves, owing to the violence, rampant ambition, and domineering arrogance of the Romish hierarchy and priesthood, the silence of the English laity under which has led to the impression that the old Anglican spirit, which extorted and secured the rights and liberties of England alike from despotic Monarchs and ambitious Pontiffs, is in the present day sinking into Irish submission and mansuetude under the imperious supremacy of priestly rule.

Lord Arundell declares that during the last 200 years the heads of the Romish Church, and I am led to infer from his observations the clergy of the communion of which he is a member, have abstained from interfering in political affairs. The assertion has caused no little astonishment, as well as ridicule and amusement, in Roman Catholic Continental circles, and, as it would be equally reprehensible, and unjust to suppose an English peer and gentleman of high character and distinguished and ancient lineage could allow himself to be simply actuated by the hateful doctrines of Liguori, according to which falsehood and deceit are meritorious, it can only be presumed that his Lordship's education in reference to history has been extremely defective, and that during the period he adverts to he is but little acquainted with the events that have occurred in France, Italy, Germany, Belgium, and almost every country in Europe, although in the former kingdom, during the reign of Louis XIV., a total separation from the Papacy had very nearly occurred, while in reference to the last it is notorious that during the recent elections in Belgium, the incidents leading to which brought the country almost to the verge of revolution, the pulpit in many parts of the kingdom was desecrated into a political tribune in which invective, anathema, and a general virulence of language were indulged in that could not have been surpassed by the worst excesses of any Democratic Convention, while in the city of Bruges a scene occurred, headed by some members of the priesthood, arising from the funeral of a lamented English lady, the widow of an esteemed Belgian functionary, that in unchristian malignity and rancourous animosity would have disgraced the worst annals of Paganism itself, the incident eliciting from the Burgomaster, M. de Boeval, a castigatien as well merited as it was severe, and as truly Christian in feeling as it was in accordance with justice and reason.

Perhaps, however, the "religious (?)" feeling existing on the part of the hierarchy and priesthood and their followers in Belgium cannot be better exemplified than in the incident which recently occurred at Tournai, where the bishop of that diocese refused to permit a procession to pass by the statue erected to commemorate the heroic and high-minded Princess d'Espinay, whose memory must ever live enshrined in the annals of her country. This lady was a devoted Roman Catholic, but she headed and encouraged the military and townspeople in their memorable defence of the city against the army of Philip II., that pious, merciful, and truly religious Prince, during whose reign two and thirty thousand persons of both sexes perished in Belgium alone by the rack, the gibbet, and the stake (exclusive of those who died on the field). A crime of so heinous a nature could not be overlooked by so pious a prelate, in whose sentiments it is reasonable to suppose Sir George Bowyer, Dr. Manning, and others of their party, fully sympathize, although, had those gentlemen, on their conversion to Roman Catholicism, been sent with their families to Norfolk Island, there to herd with the worst description of felons and criminals, it is reasonable to suppose their reverence and admiration for the late Tuscan and Neapolitan, as well as the present Roman and Spanish, Governments, under whom such a fate would inevitably have been awarded to them had they seceded from the Roman Catholic faith instead of that of the Church of England, would have dwindled to very diminutive proportions.

Lord Arundel may possibly deem the incidents I have adverted to as having no connection with temporal and political affairs; if so, may I ask him what meaning he applies to the following passage, extraction from the Allocution of the present Pope, the commencement of the year 1861:—

"In spite of all my repeated remonstrances and protests, Roman Catholic Sovereigns and rulers still continue to employ Protestants* in their service and Government, and have even gone the length of permitting Protestant children to be educated in Roman Catholic schools."

I have spoken of the doctrines of Liguori, now openly adopted as those of Papistry, from the period between the years 1838 and 1840—the which your Roman Catholic as well as Protestant readers may not be aware are simply those of the infamous Herman Busembaum (with some few of its most hideous maxims, such as the lawfulness of King Murder, &c., suppressed), whose work was ordered towards the close of the seventeenth century, to be publicly burnt by the hangman in every city in France, and most of the Roman Catholic capitals in Europe†—and in their adoption by the generality of the Romish hierarchy and priesthood and a large proportion of the laity, Count Montalembert, in his speech at Malines last year, would most probably find an explanation of that change he openly avowed during the last 40 years had come

---

* " Others of a different faith " is the literal translation.

† They are now openly sold as the same, the *Compendium Theologiæ Moralis S. Alp. de Liguori* being printed by the Propaganda Press since the year 1846 as the *Medulla Theologiæ Moralis (!) Her. Busembaum.* Malines, published by Hancq, printer to the Pope and College of Propaganda

over the Roman Catholic world, when events in his early years spoken of with universal horror and abhorrence were now not only palliated and excused, but alluded to with satisfaction and applause! He might well give utterance to this assertion, when only a short time previous a French archbishop was only prevented by the Imperial Government from celebrating a public jubilee in commemoration of one of the worst scenes of atrocity and murder that ever disgraced human history, and which Roman Catholic writers themselves have stigmatised as having been marked with, if possible a still greater degree of perfidy and infamy than that which distinguished even the massacre of St. Bartholomew itself.

I have no wish to impugn the general spirit of charity and liberality which marked this eminent French nobleman's declaration on that occasion, but there is one point I am desirous of adverting to, which, apparently unnoticed in England at the time, should not be permitted even now to pass altogether without comment. In his speech, as reported in the French journals, Count De Montalembert is reported to have said:—"Were I required to mention the two Governments most oppressive in former and later days, I should point to that of Elizabeth in reference to the first, and Sweden in regard to the last." This observation is, to say the least, somewhat singular, considering the country and people to whom it was addressed, and the reminiscences it could not fail to revive of the tender mercies, coeval with the period, of Philip II. and his humane and meritorious deputy, the Duke of Alva, to say nothing of that equally pious Sovereign Charles IX., and the massacre of St. Bartholomew, followed by the hideous scene of murder and treachery which occurred in the south of France already adverted to, and which the meek Prelate of the Gallican (I beg pardon, the Roman Catholic Church) wished so recently to celebrate with rejoicing and thanksgiving!

Nor was Count Montalembert's assertion in reference to the present period more fortunate, since, iniquitous and tyrannical as the conduct of the Swedish Government was unquestionably in reference to its Roman Catholic converts, it at least fell immeasurably short of that of the Tuscan and Spanish rulers in regard to their now Protestant votaries, while one circumstance connected with both, of which the Count could not have been ignorant, was prudently suppressed altogether—viz., that, while in reference to the Madai family and the Spanish victims (I beg particularly to call Lord Arundel's attention to the fact) not one single Catholic voice, with the exception of Mr. Serjeant Murphy, who was exposed in consequence of the virulent abuse of the *Tablet* and other priestly organs, was publicly raised in England in condemnation of the measure, in regard to the Swedish converts a general burst of indignation arose throughout the whole of Protestant Europe, in which the noble Primate and hierarchy of the Anglican Church took the lead. What a contrast does this afford to the course pursued upon the occasion by a large number of Liberal-Conservative Roman Catholics upon the continent—in France, Italy, Germany, and Belgium!

In conclusion, I trust I may be permitted to observe that there is a work not long since published which I would venture earnestly to recommend to Lord Arundell's perusal—*Memoirs of the House of Lorraine.* The History in question, by the Baron d'Haussez, is chiefly devoted to the career of the last two Sovereigns of that race and the conquest of Alsace and its dependencies by the French. It is universally admitted that few princes have been more steadfast adherents of the Roman Catholic faith than the Duke Charles V., and yet what was the strong and impressive warning he left to his descendants, when he foresaw the alliance that would be eventually contracted by his family with the Empress Queen Maria Theresa? To venerate the Church, and honour and respect the clergy, but to take especial care they were restricted to their proper functions, the duties of religion, and not permitted to interfere either with the affairs of Government or families. Up to within the last 12 years the counsel of this wise and sagacious Prince was steadily and inflexibly adhered to; and what has been the result of a deviation from this injunction, crowned by the conclusion of the ill-omened Concordat between the Courts of Rome and Vienna, those who are acquainted with the present state of Austria and the feeling it has created, and what it was during the reign of the Emperor Francis and the administration of the late Prince Metternich can best bear witness to.

Apologizing for the length of this communication, but believing that some observations relative to the incidents adverted to. from an old continental resident and traveller, would attract in England some degree of the very deep attention they have created abroad.

I am, Sir, your most obedient servant,

TRIBUNE

Spa, Oct. 3.

THE QUEEN AND THE POPE.
TO THE EDITOR OF THE TIMES.

SIR,—Whether I am to have the last word, or Lord Oranmore, is a point which you must determine. As, however, I believe that I am in strictnesss entitled to it, I venture again to address you, as there are still some points which it is important that I should clear up.

If Lord Oranmore has been condemned to "reiteration," it is only because to the last he has refused to grasp the extended exposition of the subject under discussion which Lord Oranmore's original misinterpretation of my views rendered necessary. Still, it is natural that Lord Oranmore should hold with some tenacity to his point, and I do not complain of it. But I do complain of positive, though possibly inadvertent misstatement, as when Lord Oranmore asserts that I state "that 'difficulty in Belgium consists simply as to the liberty of creating charitable foundations,' a mild way as Roman Catholics know, of working on the weaknesses of mankind to transfer their property from themselves and their families to the Roman Catholic Church;" whereas I distinctly stated that the contest was not against a simple Act of Mortmain, which would have been adequate to " prevent the transfer of property, &c.," but against an Act which "forbids any foundation without the direct and special authorization of the Executive power;" and which confiscates the legacy to the profit (not of the family) but of the Bureau of Official Benevolence," which, in fact, would tend to substitute a system of State Charity for one of private benevolence, as in England.

In what possible way the accumulation of Church property in Piedmont justified the invasion of Romagna I am at a loss to discover, but if the absorption of the one was really required for the justification of the previous confiscation of the other, it may be ultimately found that Tenterden steeple was the cause of the Goodwin Sands, or that the " lamb " did really make the aggression upon the " wolf "

Too much property had, no doubt, accumulated in the hands of the Church in Piedmont—i e., too much for the just equilibrium of things, but in every country property will accumulate unduly according to the tendencies of thought and feeling in the people; in France in the hands of small proprietors—in England, as some think, in the hands of single proprietors, although I believe that the law which brings this about is the keystone of our institutions. But would Lord Oranmore sanction revolutions, or the breach of public faith, either in the one case or the other, as he does in Piedmont, for the mere sake of redressing the balance? No, if this tendency of things had to be checked, it ought to have been by indirect legislation or by direct negotiation.

Now, negotiation was never seriously attempted. It is true that the show of negotiation was gone through, and embassies were repeatedly sent to Rome; but as they always demanded as a preliminary condition the removal of the Archbishop of Turin from his see, a condition which it was well known could not be complied with, the subject-matter of the negotiation was never proceeded with. (Vide proofs in Sir G. Bowyer's pamphlets Rome and Sardinia.) Now, the offence of the Archbishop of Turin was his refusal of the Sacrament to the Minister Santa Rosa. The point, let me observe, is not the conduct of the Archbishop, although I believe was not in any way characterised by the violence, but whether his act was legitimately within his spiritual jurisdiction. Lord Oranmore says it was not. Well, then, either Ministers are not amenable in their private capacity to the same spiritual law as other men, or else it is for the State to decide in every case to whom the Sacrament is to be given, and from whom it is to be withheld, and, if so, the text "Whatsoever you shall bind on earth shall be bound also in Heaven, and whatsoever you shall loose, &c.," must have been addressed to the State authorities.

Lord Oranmore says he hardly knows where I should consider the misdirection of spiritual influence to begin. I am equally at a loss to know at what point he would desire State interference to stop. He certainly does not draw the line equally for Catholics and Protestants, but said in his first letter that there "were several reasons" why the convictions of Catholics in resisting the mandates of the State should be "treated differently when held by Protestants and Roman Catholics." If a forced construction of my words would make me appear the advocate of overweening ecclesiastical ambition, a simple practical application of his would, I am afraid, again involve us in all the horrors of the old *régime* of political intolerance.

I am, Sir, your obedient servant,
ARUNDELL OF WARDOUR.

Wardour Castle, Oct. 3.

THE QUEEN AND THE POPE.
TO THE EDITOR OF THE TIMES.

SIR,—The reason why I, in the first instance, replied to Lord Arundell's letters was that I deemed it most desirable that public attention should be directed to the degree of obedience which even men of his education and position feel due to the Pope and the Roman Catholic Church. Seeing how paramount is her influence with such men, I desired the public should weigh well how irresistible it must be with those less educated and more dependent. Should not, then, all Acts of Parliament tending to facilitate the extention, and all grants of public money granted directly or indirectly in aid of this system be watched with the utmost jealousy?

Lord Arundell in his letter of the 4th inst. complains that I have from the first misinterpreted his view. Nothing can be further from my intention, and I feel confident I have at least not misinterpreted what he wrote, and to keep myself right on this head I must, Sir, once again copy his statement, and then leave it to your readers to decide between us. "Undoubtedly, there will sometimes be a conflict of jurisdiction between the spiritual and temporal, principally on the debatable ground surrounding education and the family, and when it occurs it is, I hope, likely that Catholics will be found to side with God rather than man, and obey the dictates of conscience rather than the mandate of the State." However, Lord Arundell still generally acknowledges his allegiance to this authority, but pleads that it is innocuous, as for the last 200 years it has been confined in exercise to matters purely spiritual. I gave him many instances within the last few years where it appears to me quite plain that it has been exercised in matters altogether temporal and civil. He does not deny my facts, but in *all* cases arrives at the conclusion that any interference with the interests or authority of the Church of Rome is wrong! and every exercise of her authority is right! and as the one instance I gave of the extremely injurious working of the Roman Catholic system in Peidmont appears to me of itself sufficiently strong to require at least some excuse or apology for the results arrived at, and Lord Arundell's only feeling in reference to it being that his Church was quite justified, and not sinning, but sinned against, shows what power she has to warp the judgment even of her most independent followers.

I think no advantage can accrue from any further special pleading between Lord Arundell and myself on these matters, but, perhaps, you will, if you kindly give place to this letter, allow me to make a few practical deductions from our correspondence.

Of course, in such letters a question of such vast importance has been only most superficially touched upon, but I hope the views brought forward by Lord Arundell, which are undoubtedly those of his Church, and the few instances out of many which I have brought forward to show the working of the Roman Catholic system in modern times, will, in connection with your article, the articles in other influential journals, and other correspendence in your columns (especially the letter in *The Times* of the 6th inst. signed " Tribune "), awaken the attention of the public to the fact that the claims of the Roman Catholic Church to exercise an *imperium in imperio* are the same now as they have been all through her history, and that whenever she has the power she puts this claim in force with a will as relentless and results as injurious as ever.

If the public go with me in this conclusion I trust they will no longer pay attention to those sceptics and latitudinarians who designate as bigoted and narrow-minded all those who, though willing to extend the same liberty of opinion in religious matters to others which they claim for themselves, yet feel that from the principles, the organization, and power of the Roman Catholic Church they are bound in self-defence to oppose the extension of her system, as one that is not only antagonistic to, but one which cannot co-exist with freedom of thought or judgment.

I trust that the Liberal party will more clearly recognize the wide difference between doing away with Roman Catholic disabilities and encouraging Roman Catholic encroachments. I trust that that part of the Conservative body, who have not lost their Protestantism in their High Church presentiments, will not consent to accept an offensive and defensive alliance with ultramontane Roman Catholicism. I hope that neither party will, for the sake of a temporary term of power, sacrifice those great Protestant principles which are the foundation and corner stone of all our liberties. Those who do so will incur no slight responsibility, for I feel sure, not only will they before long be swept from power by the revulsion of public feeling, but once the sleeping lion of Protestantism is roused to the belief that his forbearance has been abused, and his liberality mistaken for indifference (an assertion already publicly made by some Roman Catholics), he may lash himself into a fury of intolerance, which, however lamentable, could more easily be arrived at than controlled.

This correspondence must now end.

> I remain, your very obedient servant,
> ORANMORE AND BROWNE.

Troon, Scotland, Oct. 10.

THE QUEEN AND THE POPE.
TO THE EDITOR OF THE DAILY EXPRESS.

SIR,—I observed a letter from " G " in your paper last week, quoting the speech of Dr O'Brien, of Newcastle West, Limerick. I send you an extract from a speech of his superior, Dr. Butler, Roman Catholic coadjutor Bishop of Limerick, on which Dr. O'Brien, at Newcastle, and the Roman Catholic priests generally, in this county especially, formed their addresses and held meetings for the purpose of petitioning for an alteration of the law, which meetings are illegal under an Act of Parliament passed in Dublin by the Irish House of Commons, called the Convention Act, but which the Government treated as a dead letter, it would appear, for, though it was mentioned in the papers that such meetings had taken place, and the speeches were quoted, yet no notice was taken place, and Mr. W. F. Russell, M.P. for the city of Limerick, a Protestant, was charged with the care of more than one petition urging a change of the law.

Dr. Butler said:—" We are not contented with the English Government in Ireland; we have neither love nor liking for its dealings with the Irish race, and we would look on any struggle which would raise our country to the dignity of a nation, or secure for our people honest and equitable legislation, as an effort that every good man is bound to aid and encourage." Speaking of the Fenians, he said:—" If you cannot aid them, and do not, and if you oppose them, it is not from love to the English Government or want of sympathy with them in their love for their country."

Comment is unnecessary.—Yours,

> A LAYMAN.

KILMARNOCK: PRINTED BY JAMES M'KIE, 2 KING STREET.

Printed in the United States
41662LVS00016B/22